TURNING 50 ON EL CAMINO DE SANTIAGO

Turning 50 on El Camino de Santiago

A SOLO WOMAN'S TRAVEL ADVENTURE

Janine Harrison

Rivette Press

Cover Photo by Janine Harrison

Rivette Press, 2021

Dedication

To Jackie Larson for fostering my wanderlust; Michael Poore, Jianna Harrison, Bill and Wanda Lukens, Chyanne Husar, Lynne Benson, Barbara Shoemaker, Debbie Murphy, Colleen Wells and family, and Kathy George for their support of my trip; the pilgrims I met on my El Camino de Santiago sojourn, especially those who became my "international family" and with a special thank you to Pamela Bittles; Paul Kiel and Cliff Bittles; *Globe Trekker*, Shirley MacClaine, and Cheryl Strayed for the inspiration; Mary-Tina Vrehas and Ted Kosmatka for constructive critique; Izabela Kučina for her design passion and talent and Fayth Schutter for her editing and proofreading skills; and women travel writers everywhere, who encourage me to yearn travel and be brave enough to seize every opportunity within grabbing distance.

Contents

"Travel, after all, is about people. It's about learning from locals and travelers. It's about sharing experiences, swapping stories, and human connection."

- Nomadic Matt

Prologue

I'm not going out like that, I decided.

Two of my friends who'd already turned 50 years old had entered the second half of their lives with a whimper. One hid under blankets on the couch all day and the other forbid loved ones from even mentioning the "B" word (birthday). I wanted to enter 50 with a clamor! I had *earned* 50! I was surprised to even *see* 50! If I could have walked up to and kissed 50 in greeting – and gratitude – *so* much gratitude for good health, my family, multitudinous other amazing people, and a wealth of beautiful and tragic experiences that proved exemplary teachers, I would have done so instantly.

My longing for travel was, in part, born from watching Ian Wright on *Globe Trekker*, who never said "no" to a new experience, was personable to all he met, and kept a great sense of humor, no matter what Adventure tossed his way. I laughed along with him every time his face popped up on PBS.

Sometime in the early aughts, one of my best friends, Jackie, gave me Shirley MacClaine's travel memoir, *The Camino*, for Christmas. I'd never even heard of El Camino de Santiago, but I dug into the narrative that winter all the same. MacClaine's storytelling grew a little too "out there" for me, so I never finished reading the book - however, the seed had been planted!

Within the next decade, I would read and love Cheryl Strayed's memoir, *Wild*, about her life-altering sojourn hiking the Pacific Crest Trail. After, I would add El Camino to my brain's back burner "Bucket List." But my daughter, Jianna, was still little, and I had neither the time nor money to travel, so the trip would need to wait.

Still, I could envision it: Me, walking mile after mile alone, unburdening myself of memories of abusive men who had collectively tattooed a tribal scar upon my person.

What I couldn't know then was that by the time I would board a plane for France, I would no longer yearn the journey for that reason. Nor could I have known that the reality of my hike would be considerably different than the inner quest I had imagined, yet prove just as, if not more, rewarding.

On June 29, 2018, I would fly from O'Hare to Charles De Gaulle airport, take two trains and one bus to Saint-Jean-Pied-de-Port, France, and start my hike over the Pyrenees the next day, hiking for one week. Adventures in Pamplona and Paris would follow. The succeeding chapters serve as travel memoir and guide to my solo travel journey as a middle-aged (but young in spirit!) woman celebrating life.

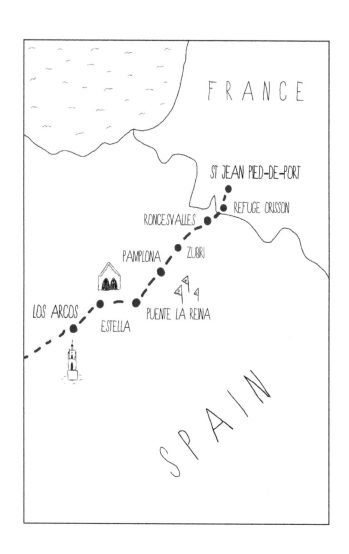

FRANCE

ST JEAN PIED-DE-PORT
REFUGE ORISSON
RONCESVALLES
ZUBRI
PAMPLONA
LOS ARCOS
PUENTE LA REINA
ESTELLA

SPAIN

One

Backpacks, Basque Country, and Beer

As I followed my map to a stone archway, I watched as locals in their Sunday best headed for morning services. I was on the lookout for stores, so that I could purchase a hiking stick, but to no avail. No businesses were open. *That's okay. I'm sure there'll be something along the way.* The air was still crisp. I strolled, knowing that I wouldn't pass this way again, wanting to take in as much of Saint-Jean as I could.

Despite the draining trip from Northwest Indiana to Saint-Jean-Pied-de-Port, France, I'd awoken in my albergue bed at 3 AM. *Wow, I did all right, considering it was my first day's hike!* I recalled walking up and up, even the pull on my calves due to the incline. *Wait a minute!* I looked at the full bunkbeds on the other side of the room – *I haven't even left yet!* It was only an anticipatory dream.

By 7:30 AM, I'd lightened my backpack, eaten a hearty breakfast with other peregrinos, said my good-byes and thank you's to host Joseph and staff at Beilari, grabbed my sack lunch, and made it to the Pilgrim's office for my second Pilgrim's Passport stamp (Beilari being the first). From a basket, I chose a large scallop shell to hang on my backpack, Paprika (so-named by my 13-year-old), signifying the pilgrimage.

As a U.S. citizen in 2018, I felt it necessary to weasel "and Trump is NOT my president" into the conversation, which made the two French folks behind the office counter chuckle. I further shared my dream about completing the hike to Orisson, the day's destination, halfway up the French side of the Pyrenees. A volunteer responded, "Today is not a dream!"

I was in the Basque province at the foot of the mountains and had stayed overnight in a stone house that had been built toward the end of the Middle Ages, upper story and shutters painted the traditional white and red. Inside was a sturdy, dark wood staircase, built-in bookcase beneath; regional map on one wall; container for hiking staffs and hats in a corner. Upstairs, I'd shared a small bedroom decorated with framed El Camino scenes and hiking ornamentation with two women, a German and a Swede.

Beilari was in the walled-in section of the city – with narrow, medieval cobblestone streets, stone edifice lined – and situated directly on the historic Rue de la Citadelle. The buildings, red and white trimmed, with carved, baroque balconies and overhangs, silently signaled their approval, guided me, as I walked. It was a charming town founded in the 12th century, the old capital of Base-Navarre. And, it marked the start of the Camino Frances.

When I crossed the stone bridge over River Nive, framed by buildings from a bygone time, mist rising off the water, another bridge followed by trees in the distance, I felt transported. I exhaled. *I made it – my sojourn is starting*! Exhilaration that only a solo travel adventure can bring burbled within me. I'm sure my eyes shined.

I reached a brass triangle bearing an engraved scallop shell affixed to the stone street, indicating the way. After taking a photo of my feet before this arrow, I walked through an outer suburb, becoming farms, housing increasingly sparse, heading for the Pyrenean foothills.

*

True to my American values, I couldn't help but wonder why no one had anything for sale at their property entrances alongside the roadside – like hiking sticks! *What missed com-*

mercial opportunities! You'd never see that in the United States! Perhaps it was because it was a Sunday and the French took their day of worship and rest seriously? Perhaps they never opened kiosks? I don't know. The only example of business I found, which seemed *so* out of place that it made me smile, was a vending machine inside of a shallow wooden enclosure, a green bench nearby. While sitting down for a moment, a tall, fair German father and teenage son duo, Alexander and Max, approached, smiling. They spoke English; we parted laughing several minutes' later.

The sun was rising, and I pushed up my hoodie sleeves. *What a trip I've already had!*

In true Janine fashion, it started with a comedy of errors. The afternoon before last, my husband Mike's Jeep overheated on the way to O'Hare. He slowed to baby his four-wheeled baby. "Sorry about this," he said, frowning at the gauges.

"Go to the international gates," I soon said, pointing to a lane.

It was the wrong gate, and we ended up waiting in a full taxi lane.

By the time we corrected the problem, I was running even later.

When I climbed out of the two-door vehicle and grabbed my backpack to yank it out from behind the passenger seat, a keychain with an emergency alarm function I'd attached, just in case, went off, echoing throughout the terminal car port. Simultaneously, one leg on the pair of old hiking poles attached to the pack decided to extend for no reason whatsoever. Mike left, and after silencing the alarm, I struggled with the pole. I couldn't re-collapse the end. I approached a young stranger waiting for a ride, but he fared no better. Frustrated, I realized, while walking inside, that security might think that my alarm was a bomb and that there was no way the poles would pass through the x-ray machine with the leg out, so I chucked both items into the nearest trash can and headed for check in.

"Group A may now board."

I walked the covered ramp length and boarded my United flight. As a Christmas present, a set of my in-laws treated me to my first (and likely last!) first-class, international, roundtrip flight, and to say the very least, it was lovely! I was one fortunate and grateful daughter-in-law. And, at the moment, I couldn't imagine how much first-class accommodations would mean to me on the flight home.

Essentially, I became a very comfy pea in a pod, surrounded by every imaginable need or want. Ordering a Heineken, I had it in hand as travelers passed by on the way to their economy seats. I had anticipated being surrounded by affluent types: you know – CEO's and Stepford wives and public figures. Instead, the woman who sat across from me was unexpected. I glanced her way, noting her bibbed overalls and neon green Crocs, which she soon slid off, revealing white ankle socks.

"Can I have champagne?" she asked the flight attendant. "I read that we could order champagne for free." She had snowy hair, and a portion of her face was bruised, as if she were either healing from a good wallop to the eye or had fallen hard. She smiled.

"It is free for ya'll," the hostess assured her and brought a glass. The passenger and I smiled at one another, briefly chit-chatted, and settled into our hulls.

I couldn't help but wonder about her back story. Was she dying and this was her "last hurrah"? She seemed a hearty soul – a sturdy, farm woman, if I were to guess; I didn't get a "death vibe" from her, but that didn't necessarily mean anything. She seemed definitely to be celebrating something well deserved and a long-time coming. To a lesser extent, I could relate.

The attendant herself was no "spring chicken." But that didn't stop her from wearing heels well. A warm woman, she took great care of us during the night. She asked about my trip, and when I told her that I was planning to hike El Camino for a week, turning 50 years old on day seven, she replied, "Honey, I've been working for two years longer than you've been on this Earth!" Lowering her voice, she continued, "The secret is to keep moving."

Morning came. I glimpsed fields in France through my window, which looked less "patchwork quilt-like" than the U.S.'s - these meandered more.

Just before landing, the attendant handed me a gift – a bag of four travel-size Bailey's Irish Creams! "For your birthday," she said. "Enjoy your hike!"

Just then, the older passenger piped up, asking, "How do I get from the airport to Paris?"

*

I started ascending the mountain. Each hill and plateau brought a new green, bucolic scene, one I often paused to admire. I discovered a tiny white Virgin Mary statue in the shade of a tree, surrounded by stones. Ivy wrapping its way around a fence post. As the sun rose farther in the sky and my 16 lb. pack grew heavier as the road steepened, I took off my hoodie and tied it around my waist. The climb was getting tougher, and I wasn't feeling that great. In fact, I was growing sicker by the minute and often, due to the increased elevation, had to stop to catch my breath.

Before the trip, I'd starting walking longer distances, two miles here, three miles there, simultaneously breaking in my hiking shoes, as recommended. I'd recruited a couple of friends, Barb and Debbie, to join me on the "Three Dune Challenge" along the Lake Michigan shoreline, too, so that my practice wasn't entirely on flat land. I'd have trained harder had I planned to complete the entire trek. However, I began to wonder: *Am I a fool for thinking I could do this with so little training?*

How much farther? I sounded like my daughter when she was little: "Are we there yet?"

To be frank, I have anxiety. Although I'd been on trips throughout the United States as well as to Haiti and Mexico by myself, my nervousness had worsened at the thought of having to take an international flight, followed by two train rides and a bus ride, with the three ground segments located in France where I didn't speak the language, consecutively, within a 24-hour span. The mere thought exhausted me. Even though all went well, the previous day's heightened mental and emotional states had zapped my physical reserve.

Charles de Gaulle airport had been very cool – people movers in translucent tubes shooting off in all directions. Very *The Jetsons*. I also appreciated the bicycle-powered, cell phone charging stations. *Why don't we have these in the U.S.?!?* Renewable energy *and* exercise – you can't beat that!

Toilettes cost 0,70€. I hadn't seen a pay toilet since I'd been in a bus station in Atlanta on my 1986 high school senior class trip to Disney World, where they'd cost a dime. One girl paid and then, my classmates and I simply held the door open for one another from there on out. It wasn't that we didn't each have ten cents – it was the principle of the thing, damn it!

After using the bathroom, I stood at the sink, trying to freshen up: comb, toothbrush, deodorant. A woman near my height and age, with a gazillion long red and pink braids and a nose piercing, approached me. She hurled her words: "I'm a pilgrim, too! This is my fourth time doing the Camino. Will you watch this?" Setting down her pack, she disappeared into a stall as I nodded.

After, we introduced ourselves. She was Pamela, originally from Canada but a recent immigrant, with her husband, Cliff, to the Dominican Republic.

A few minutes after we parted ways, I headed to my train with what I thought was my advance purchase train ticket. She glimpsed me en route and pointed out that I still had to retrieve the *actual* ticket – what I was holding was merely the confirmation; she guided me to an automated machine and walked me through the process.

Since I'd visited Haiti twice, we compared notes about Hispaniola while on the platform. We had assigned seats in separate cars, though, so soon split up again.

It was a bullet train – my first! While passing a train going in the opposition direction or greenery growing close to the tracks, images manifested as sheets of blue or green horizontal lines like something out of *Dr. Who*! My ears even popped a couple of times.

After detraining, Pamela and I chatted. When we said good-bye to board our second train, she yelled over her shoulder, "I'll buy you a beer in Bayonne!" We had a short layover there. I looked forward to it while enjoying this slower ride, gazing out the window at farmland, small adobe houses with clay tile roofs, a group of shacks, and a couple of dilapidated mansions that I tried to imagine in their glory. *I wonder who lived there?*

Pamela and I quickly spotted one another at the Bayonne station and crossed the street to an Irish pub, where we clinked glasses, drank our beer, and chatted at an outdoor table with other pilgrims, mainly a large, jovial group from Ireland.

I'd be remiss if I didn't say a few words about Bayonne, my first taste of Southwest France and the capital of French Basque countryside. A colossal clock tower perched on the train station like a Peregrine Falcon, Gare de Bayonne, built in the 19th century. A medieval stronghold with cobbled streets, it was charming.

We parted, Pamela to a third train, and me, to a bus. On that final leg, the farther Southwest I traveled, the nicer the suburbs became.

Then - at long last – Saint-Jean-Pied-de-Port!

I grabbed Paprika and rushed toward the exit, the bus having run later than expected. After taking a photo of the street map posted at the stop, I started to walk. A few blocks later, growing concerned, I stopped, read a street sign, and checked it against my image.

"Hey! Are you lost, little girl?"

I turned. Across the street was Pamela, walking and smiling. She beckoned; I joined. We made a sharp turn into a seemingly hidden passageway within brick, leading to the historic portion of the city. I'm not sure if I would've found it without her. Heck, I could still be standing there now! After glancing at my albergue address, Pamela dropped me literally at the front door. "Thanks again!" I smiled.

"Where are you staying tomorrow?" she asked. "Orisson or Roncesvalles?"

"Orisson."

She hadn't made reservations but was hoping it wasn't already full, so she could stay, too.

"If so, it's *my* turn to buy *you* a beer!" I called over my shoulder as we separated.

"Put your pack here," said an employee. I set it down and followed the man to a stone-walled patio dining room filled with greenery. He directed me to a seat. Dinner was about to commence.

About 30 of us pilgrims sat around the two long tables. Host Joseph called us "family." He served sweet wine and then announced, "We're going to go around the room. Please tell us your name, country of origin, and reason for hiking El Camino de Santiago."

While most folks spoke in English, French, and Spanish, I also heard other languages. Sometimes, translations followed.

A man from Puerto Rico, I learned, would be turning 50 on the French Way, too. I smiled in his direction as I gave my similar introduction. He grinned.

I sat with Kristen and Stacy, two female OB/gynecologists from Chicago (small world!); a young, powerfully-built woman from Deusseldorf, whom I would bunk across from that night and who would walk all of the way to Roncesvalles the next day; a young Hungarian woman; and a Swedish woman I would also bunk with and get to know over time.

We had a white bean soup, salad, and frittata, which were delicious, more wine, and a yogurt-dessert thing (that no one at our table liked), then went to bed. This "early to bed, early to rise," would be my first taste of the typical pilgrim lifestyle.

*

Toward the end of my hike to Orisson, the combination of airplane food, beer, wine, French food, and jet lag, along with my anemia, under hot sun in high elevation, would cause me to "pull over" to the trailside, clammy and chilly, feeling as if I were going to vomit.

However, that did not stop me from noticing the view had gone from pastoral to breathtaking - something I would appreciate even more the next morning! I observed everything from mist draping the valley to flowers growing from the mountainside at once so beautiful and fierce and tenacious that you wanted to give them a hug and a medal at the same time.

I also met Linda from Montreal, an older man from Japan, and Marie from Paris (who, upon running across me a second time on the trail, asked, "Are you all right?"). For her, the trek seemed but a leisurely stroll.

Eventually, I spied Orisson – a sight for sore everything! – which renewed my strength enough to walk the final kilometer.

I'd hiked approximately 9 kilometers, not a lot, but mostly going up, Up, UP!

At check-in, I was handed a token for a five-minute shower. And I *needed* a shower, needed a shower like I had never before needed one! I planned my stall time, so that if I ran out of water I could still wash my face and hair in the sink. Exhausted though I was, I somehow managed a thorough scrub before the spray thinned to drizzle then nothing. Fortunately, this would be the only place I stayed that used a token system.

I settled in – this room was larger; Linda had the lower bunk of our bed and across from us was a nice couple, Karen and Cort, from Kansas City. The two OB's from Chicago shared a third bunk bed and two other pilgrims, a fourth, on the far end.

After scarfing down my sandwich from Joseph's kitchen and exploring the albergue – the only option halfway up the Pyrenees – complete with restaurant/bar and outdoor seating overlooking the green-blue-gray peaks and valleys below, I found Pamela and bought us both a big Eki mug of beer. We proceeded to talk non-stop for two straight hours.

The journey of **100** miles...

Crossing River Nive, leaving Saint-Jean-Pied-de-Port

En route to Orisson, Pyrenees

One: Travel Tidbits

Resources

Kelly, Gerald. *Camino de Santiago: Practical Preparation and Background*. 2nd edition, Self-Published, 2015. (Among other pieces of information that you will glean is to order your pilgrim's passport well in advance of your trip!)

What Worked

- Scouring Gerald Kelly's guidebook first, roughly planning my route and making an initial supplies list in a dedicated journal
- Joining a local Camino group and attending their workshop on purchasing and stocking a backpack

What I Would Do Differently

- Spend a second night in Saint-Jean-Pied-de-Port, France, to recuperate from international travel and have time to explore and enjoy the historic city before setting out on my journey

Two

Royalty, Route to Roncesvalles, and Rituals

Pamela and I chose to sit indoors, out of the sun. We had the dining room, with its wooden beams and tables, cream walls, and generous natural light, practically to ourselves. And, we talked about everything.

"Mike writes literary and science fiction novels."

"Cliff loves sci-fi!"

"And on my second trip to Haiti…"

"I opened a salon in the DR, and…"

We compared dogs.

We talked husbands some more. Mine was writing royalty; Pamela's Cliff was an actual Irish prince, whose family had left for Canada during The Troubles. He referred to his beloved as "Princess Pamela."

Our chatter continued until our draft drinking, on top of our uphill trek, prompted pre-dinner naps.

When I entered the dining room that evening, Pamela called me over and introduced me to a mother and daughter from Denmark, Marianne and Michelle, who were fluent in English. We four enjoyed each other from the get-go.

As with the previous night, the full room of pilgrims was asked to introduce ourselves. Not as many hikers were on religious journeys as I had anticipated, but many individuals were on spiritual quests, including Marie from France, whom, it turned out, was a young widow trying to gain purchase on what it meant to continue life without her husband by her side. *Just like Pam.* At least two pilgrims had recovered from cancer, Marianne being one, and were checking this item off of their "bucket list." Others were walking for reasons involving weight loss or general health. A few children were hiking, too. One boy said, "I'm Cayden, and I'm nine, and this is my first time walking the Camino."

Another boy explained in Spanish that he was just in it "for the food."

Partway through dinner, it started to storm. Suddenly, huge hail stones pummeled the windows and ground. We wondered what this would mean for our next day's journey.

Pamela told me that she'd had her backpack driven to Orisson and was having it delivered to our next albergue, a monastery, as well. She gave herself time to become accustomed to the hike before adding the pack weight. After feeling so nauseous earlier and with the onset of ominous weather, I decided to make a ride reservation for Paprika before returning to my bunk.

*

I'd started reading Elizabeth Gilbert's novel, *Eat, Pray, Love*, which I'd picked up at a library book sale and had a related thought while hiking: *No need to meditate today. I don't need to check in with my body – it's checking in with me!*

I slept hard until about 3 AM, when Brain decided that I should set an intention on each day of the hike a la *Eat, Pray, Love*. My intention for day two would be to let go of bullies and remember how well I've been loved throughout my life and how blessed I am that the latter outweighed the former.

I fell back to sleep and awoke again a few hours later. After I was ready, one of the first things I did was to text Mike to announce that I'd beat him to our seventh wedding anniversary

– July 2nd - and would celebrate us at the top of the Pyrenees later that day!

Outside, bird song framed the majestic view, lower mountains seeming to fold in toward one another, separated only by lakes of mist. Such grandeur! It was perhaps at that moment that my shoulders started to relax.

After breakfast, all of the peregrinos seemed to be leaving at about the same time, more resembling the beginning of a race than a solo hike. I saw Pamela outside; she said, "I'm a slow hiker, so don't wait for me – I'll see you at the monastery or maybe on the trail."

Nodding, off I strode.

This day's hike proved longer but gentler, and I felt well the whole hike. Crickets were my morning soundtrack. I greeted and passed the OB/Gyn's, trudging in sync, hiking poles in hand, chatting all the while. Fog nestled in the mountains and the gray sky threatened downpour. I donned my orange raincoat (from Cabela's clearance room - not my first color choice, but the price was right.) The OB/Gyn's later commented, "Whenever we checked to see what lay ahead on the route, we just looked for your jacket!"

Pilgrims walked in groups, pairs, and alone at different times, leapfrogging one another as we aimed for the summit. This would typify a given day.

Mid-morning, I heard the sound of bells and soon came upon the source – animals: cows and long-haired sheep grazing grass and drinking from a stream. They weren't fenced in, and no shepherd was in sight. One poor sheep wore an enormous brass bell, inverted-hourglass shaped and so long that it nearly touched the ground. I wondered what the poor ewe had done to be sentenced to such a weighty charm. It was definitely on house arrest. *Is it a flight risk?*

I rounded a corner and a horse crossed my path. *Is that good luck?*

Eventually, I saw a shepherd with three dogs. The man and I nodded in greeting.

Along the way were cairns, too – solemn, like miniature pine trees, made from rocks. I knew from reading that many such structures were built by pilgrims as memorials to lost loved ones.

As I walked, I mentally reinforced learned lessons, determined to have increased control in my second "half?" of life, something that I had already been working on with improved success for over a decade. I made a list: 1. No co-dependency or displaced loyalty to men or jobs, 2. Better boundaries, 3. No feeling guilty saying "no," 4. Be true to my intuition – my "self" – and not care what others think, and 5. Speak up when something needs to be said. As an ACoA (Adult Child of an Alcoholic), I'd grown up a people pleaser, a workaholic, a perfectionist. Slowly, I healed my way from co-dependent to empath and toward more work-life balance, especially as a Mom and wife who wanted to make as many wonderful family memories as possible while we were all together and healthy. I'd be lying if I didn't admit that time's ever-present tick was beginning to boom.

Pamela and I met one another at a food truck in the middle of nowhere – the only such vehicle I would see on the entire journey. By this time, the sun had decided to clock in to the sky. We continued our walk together, along with a teacher, Jennifer, originally from New Jersey, who'd moved to Canada. As we passed stone storm shelters built for shepherds, Pamela told us about her first trek. "I'd reached about here and it started thunder storming. The lightning was so close – I was really scared and didn't know what to do! A couple in a car going the opposite way offered to take me back to Saint-Jean-Pied-de-Port, so I got in."

She started her hike anew the next day, an acceptable setback considering she could have lost her life.

The trees were fun. Some straightened their backs, attempting to be the closest to the sun. Others, on occasion, clasped leaves over the road, providing us shade.

My favorite scene from the morning, though, was without a doubt a large crop of rocks that looked as if a giant with a brush had splattered them with white paint. (I don't know why they looked that way. I could look it up, but that would take away from the magic. Don't you think?)

Sometimes Jennifer walked with us but not always. At one point, Pamela and I needed a break, and a boulder alongside the path proved just the perch for us. We soon declared ourselves a greeting committee of two and, whenever pilgrims hiked by, beamed wide smiles and bellowed "Good Morning!" Before long, we'd given our salutation in English, French, Spanish, and German.

Late morning, Pamela filmed me singing and dancing a rendition of "The Hills are Alive" from *The Sound of Music*. It was laughably bad, but I didn't care. It had to be done - the moment demanded it!

When we finally reached the peak of the Pyrenees, we took in the view, appearing equal with the fleecy clouds. Pamela took a photo of me toasting "salúte" with my water bottle to Mike for our anniversary, which I then texted. Several of us from Orisson took a photo together on a wooden bench. After ten or so minutes of rest and chit-chat, the group, including Pamela, left without me. Pamela knew that I had some private business to handle.

Around my neck, I wore an urn necklace, carrying ashes of my best guy friend, Paul, who'd died rather suddenly that January at age 50, leaving behind wife, Pam, and adolescents, Matthew and Joshua. From the time we were teenagers, Paul and I had been buddies. We'd laughed and had many adventures together, and he'd been my rock when I might otherwise have blown away. So, I constructed a small cairn, surrounding it with yellow wildflowers in such a pattern that they resembled sun beams, thanked him for always being "tops" in my book – tears threatening all the while – and started to unscrew the lid of the ornate silver cannister to sprinkle him – only, he wouldn't come out!

Pam had told me that the funeral director recommended lightly gluing the inside of the top to secure it, which I had done, using Elmer's Wood Glue, and well, in the contest of me vs. lid, the score was: Elmer's 1, Janine 0.

Paul loved to fish. *I guess he wants to be by a river.*

I thought back to a morning fishing trip to the Kankakee river in Illinois. Paul and I had started driving before the sun even brewed her first cup a Joe and her lowest beams cast into near-tranquil waters. Within five minutes, Paul caught a five-pound cat! We just knew we'd be hauling in fish all morning! Then, over the next few hours – nothing! Not. one. bite. As noon approached, we stowed away our gear. "Wanna get a beer?" Paul asked.

We wound up at a local tavern for the afternoon, judging a pickled egg contest between bartender contestants and shooting pool, fairly evenly matched.

It had been a difficult year so far. The previous December, I'd stepped down from my college English teaching position of 15 years and was entering uncharted territory as a full-time freelance writer. It was scary. At times, I felt perhaps I'd forgotten to pack my self-confidence in a banker's box with my books when I moved out of my campus office. Or, maybe it was still packed away somewhere? Then, one January night Pam called with the news that Paul was gravely ill. I spent part of the evening thirty minutes away, driving past my and Paul's houses in our adjacent hometowns, just to feel closer to him. Returning, I imbibed beer like in days of old.

Too soon, I found myself driving to Northwestern Hospital in Chicago to say good-bye. I'd actually googled how to say good-bye to someone who was dying. I'd been at deathbeds before, but this time I wanted to be prepared for our final exchange. But I couldn't be. Communication was unidirectional.

I joked as always, I squeezed his hand, I told him how much he was loved, I kissed his cheek. As I left his bedside, I tried getting him to look at me. Madonna, vogue, I struck a pose, then another. But Paul, senses shuttering, had already lost his sight.

Within days, he was dead.

I helped Pam to plan the funeral and gave my eulogy with only one catch in my throat as I spoke. My interior monologue was *not* a match.

I settled into an anxiety-riddled fog, low energy, little concentration, much comfort food-eating, for the remainder of winter and all of spring. It seemed impossible to me that Paul could be gone just like *that.*

Paul was my "go to" guy for a shoulder to cry on when my boyfriends were being shitty, which they usually were because men were the gaping chink in my armor. He was also my escort when I wasn't dating anyone. We both worked in the Chicago Loop while we were in our early-20's. One night, he met me at a train station to accompany me to an work affair at a swanky bar in an upscale neighborhood. He took me through lower Wacker Drive to get there and as we passed the tent towns of the homeless, every few yards one of my black, stiletto heels would catch in the cobblestone. I'd give him my 'Really, Paul?' look, and he'd laugh. Before I knew it, we were downing free cocktails and slithery raw oysters and shooting pool among top advertising elites. I was a lowly editorial assistant at a trade magazine start-up, and this was our first networking affair. I'd just earned my first bi-line. The whole evening felt surreal! On the train ride home to our south suburbs, Paul handed me his copy of our new, four-color *Chicago Advertising & Media* publication and asked, "May I have your autograph?"

He was the first to ask.

It wasn't all YA angst and alcohol, fishing and frolicking, though. As we grew older, life got real – more real than we could ever imagine. Paul and Pam's one-year-old son, Matthew, was diagnosed with neuroblastoma in his head. One night, I visited the family in the hospital, brightly-colored Mickey Mouse plushy in hand. Paul walked me back to the lobby. I'd never seen his eyes look so carved out. In the lobby, he pulled out his hip flask and offered me a swill.

"We almost lost him…"

I took a gulp, maybe three, with him.

But Matthew survived and thrived, like one of those tough, tenacious flowers I'd seen rising from the French side of the mountain.

I rose and started to wend my way down the other mountain side. Since I was alone, I talked out loud to Paul. Anger and lamentation over his premature death, many thank you's and much love, ended with, "Your family is doing all right, Paul. They're going to be okay. I'll do what I promised and help to take care of them."

Paul's brother, Mark, also made this vow. Paul's family and I couldn't know then that he wouldn't be able to keep it. Within months of Paul's funeral, Mark would take a job doing interior home remodeling for a single mother, who'd left her abusive husband. While her children were away and Mark was installing cabinets, the estranged partner would enter the home and knife them both to death, hours' later, turning himself in to the police. Uncle Mark was gone, the brothers reunited.

I let go of my grief as best I could and switched focus to my own life, my own approach to age 50.

Upon reaching this incredible spot, like an unofficial, organic overlook, no one in sight in any direction, I spoke to the universe: "I'm grateful for everyone and everything – most of all my family and all the other beautiful people in my life. Thank you for my good brain and good health!"

I'm sure there was more, but that was the gist.

It felt wonderful to give my thanks aloud.

Within half an hour, I'd caught up to Pamela and company, and we crossed into Spain, reaching Albergue de Peregrinos Orreaga Roncasvalles in the early afternoon. We'd walked about 17 km, completing the initial stage. Before checking in, we sat on a café patio and toasted with tall, cold drafts of cerveza de Estrella Galicia.

*

Paprika and I were reunited at the registration desk. The monastery was surprisingly clean, modern, and efficiently run. With three floors, it contained one of the two largest dorms I'd stay in, and what I appreciated most was a locker with a key. Much of El Camino revolved around trusting fellow pilgrims, but the American in me liked locks – locks reduced anxiety.

In what would become routine, the first item on my (and most pilgrims') "to do's" involved a much-needed shower. For me, this was followed by journaling and napping. Then, I walked around the grounds and snapped a few photos: the original stone cathedral with bell; the new one with Biblical scene depicted above the double doors; a sculpture that looked like beef jerky in the form of a fruit rollup; and red roses contrasting magnificently with the sandstone wall behind them.

Built as the Roncesvalles Hospitality Institution around 1127 to help pilgrims traveling the St. James' Way, the monastery had become a heritage site. Roncesvalles, itself, was the site of a famous battle in 778 A.D., in which Charlemagne's rear army was defeated by the Basques. This battle formed the basis for the legend of the hero Roland, recounted in epic tales.

Before long, it was time for dinner. Unlike before, we stood in line and waited to be seated in an elegant dining room. Pamela and I were led to a round table, where we sat with Marie from France, whom we got to know better, and three women from Italy. I enjoyed discussing my Italian honeymoon with them (unable to say enough about gelato, glorious, delicious gelato!). Our meal arrived in courses. Akin to a fancy restaurant experience, it felt funny to sit there, wearing a tank top, shorts, and sandals, but when in Rome... (or Spain).

Marie, we learned, owned an architectural firm in Paris; she and her female colleagues mainly took on exterior design projects, such as public parks. Since my niece, Chyanne, was an architect with her own Chicago firm, we traded notes.

The conversation became more relaxed as wine flowed and Marie made a comparison of my and Pamela's hiking, but needed help with her English. "You know – the animal with a house on its back?"

Snails!

Standing at about 5'3 apiece, it was our short legs – according to Marie, we walked as slow as snails! Somehow, the joke evolved, and we became the "Snail Sisters" for the remainder of our trek and beyond.

After we finished eating, we walked to the cathedral for the Pilgrim's Blessing, given in Spanish. Although not Catholic and with Spanish skills only good enough to catch every few words, I'm not sorry that I attended. Men in formal clergy wear, adorned in green and gold, as conduits from the holy to the human. A blessing never hurts. I believe in the power of prayer – that concentrated energy of the universe.

Bed, cruel mistress, soon beckoned.

Top of the Pyrenees, France: Sophie (Sweden), Jennifer, Me, and Stefan

Cows, grazing and lazing

Two: Travel Tidbits

Resources

Brierley, John. *Camino de Santiago: St. Jean Pied de Port –
      Santiago de Compostela.* Camino Guides, Dyke, 2018.

What Worked

○ Owning a cell phone case with charging ability. In albergues, most pilgrims want to charge electronics, so
  outlets are at a premium. Fortunately, a friend, Kathy,
  gave me a charging case for my cell phone as a birthday
  present. For this reason, I did not miss any Pyrenees
  photo opp's.

What I Would Do Differently

○ Request my backpack be delivered on day one to Orisson, a steeper climb, instead of day two, to Roncesvalles
○ Purchase a better solar charger. The inexpensive one
  that I bought worked slowly at best. Given a re-do, I'd
  read reviews and perhaps consider: "You get what you
  pay for."

Three

Plans, Pinchos in Pamplona, and Pizza

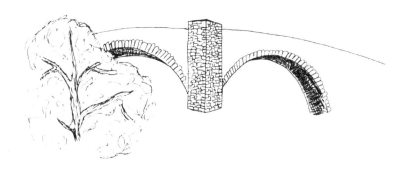

Since we hiked at roughly the same pace, Pamela and I stayed together after Roncesvalles. Our next day's trek was to Zubiri, through farmland and forests. It felt wonderful to be in the shade and breathe in the fresh scent of trees, critter sounds playing in the background. Walks through woods have always served me well, mentally, emotionally. Studies support the benefit of nature hikes. And forests seem sacred somehow.

I snapped a photo of the side of a building, which, in large letters, read, "Welcome to the Basque Country," followed in smaller print by: "Kultura Sentitu – Feel the Culture – Siente la Cultura – La Cultura Sentir – Sentire la Cultura." It announced the Spanish counterpart to what we'd already experienced in France.

A day for lingering, I took a photo of a sign, indicating that Ernest Hemingway had traveled the route. Later, in a town, I snapped another, of a Hemingway quote written in Spanish on a chalkboard: "It takes two years to learn to speak and sixty to learn to be silent."

Pamela and I passed Jennifer and Camila, an artist from Brazil whom we'd met the previous afternoon, soaking their feet in a stream. We toured an old cemetery within stone walls of tatty trees and weighty cross tombstones.

Though flatter, the terrain wasn't level, and the hike was longer – 21.9 kilometers – the last downhill slope filled with loose rocks. I'd never had knee trouble, but this portion proved painful to a frontal area just beneath my kneecaps, one more than the other. Since I didn't have poles and Pamela did, she walked ahead of me, and I simply concentrated on following in her footsteps. I was thankful for this because she went down at a rather quick, steady clip, and if I had been on my own, I'd have been in danger of overthinking my footing. Toward the bottom of the slope, I limped to the extent that she loaned me a pole to help compensate for the worse leg. We entered Zubiri, our destination, and Pamela approached a local woman. "¿Me puede recomendar un lugar para quedarse?"

As it turned out, she let rooms. After grabbing keys, she escorted us around the corner to an apartment. For 20€ apiece, we had a bedroom with a window that looked out upon a hill filled with sheep; access to a kitchen that also included a washer and a dryer; and a semi-private bathroom. Score! After lovely (and I do mean *lovely*!) showers, we found ourselves at a local restaurant, drinking beer and eating Pilgrims' meals (which were discounted options) with Marianne and Michelle and Alexander and Max from Germany as well as Sonia and nine-year-old Theo – a mother and son from California, traveling in a party of four (Sonia's mother and seven-year-old son, James, were resting in their albergue). Chatting and laughing, we dawdled for an extra hour.

After, Pamela and I slept so hard in our twin beds that you'd have thought they were king-sized pillow tops and all our lives, we'd slumbered on mats unrolled on dirt.

The next day, we would hike to Pamplona, our first city on the French Way. Ernest Hemingway, who'd spent considerable time there, had written one of its fine cafés into his novel, *The Sun Also Rises*, and this English major aimed to have a beer and pinchos there! (Little would I know then that I was going to stalk Hemingway's ghost through Europe!)

*

By this time, Pamela had started a WhatsApp thread, and we and others collected pilgrims' phone numbers as we hiked. Everyone was soon aware that a "Pinchos Pub Crawl in Pamplona" was in the works for evening. (Yes, my event title – like the alliteration?)

Pamela and I had fallen into a routine. Due to our petite statures, we left a little earlier in the morning than our taller counterparts, so we could still reach our end points by early afternoon before the heat became difficult to bear. Sometimes, it was still dark outside when we exited that night's albergue. Pamela had a head lamp, so she'd take the lead. I followed, sometimes using my cell phone flashlight to see the path. Air would be crisp but in walking, we'd warm quickly. And the only sounds were those of birds planning their day and our in-sync footfalls. We, Snail Sisters, an army of two.

An hour or so into our hike, we would usually pass through a town that offered either a sit-down breakfast at a restaurant, often a Tortilla Española, or a convenience store, so that we could grab breakfast and lunch items to go.

I would continue to set intentions each day, concentrating on them in early mornings while we silently marched. When we did talk, as happened increasingly as a given day unfurled, my hiking partner and I unpacked our lives to show one another. While she was raised in Canada and I, in the United States, and she was a few years my junior, the similarities were striking. Both our lives had been arduous, including physical abuse, and we had survived and become stronger in the process. Pamela was on El Camino this time to process having been primary caregiver for and having lost both in-laws, who'd been like actual parents to her, within the last two years.

We'd also developed great senses of humor, likely as coping mechanisms, as we'd grown older, so we laughed – a lot.

We were goofy in the same ways. Once, while walking with Marianne, Michelle, and Marie, I told Pamela, "I'm planning to write a book about this journey."

Immediately, she leapt ahead of the book and planned who would star in the film. Getting ahead of the group, she flipped around to walk backward so she could announce the idea and declare, "I want Julia Roberts to play me!"

"Dibs on Reese Witherspoon!" I chimed. (If she was good enough for Cheryl Strayed, then she was certainly good enough for me!)

"What about for Marie?" asked Pamela. We studied our pretty, young friend and decided she was a dead ringer for Anne Hathaway.

As we hiked, Marianne confessed that she didn't know American movie stars. (And why should she? She lived in Denmark!) The sound of crunching gravel filled our conversational void.

"Sandra Bullock?" Pamela suggested at last.

"I want a big chest," Marianne declared.

We decided that Pamela Anderson could do a boob cameo.

Michelle, Danish, but ethnically half-Middle Eastern, was a bit more challenging. Hmm... We eventually determined that Megan Fox or America Ferrera would suffice.

Before moving on, we added Gerard Butler. We didn't know an actual pilgrim that he would play. We just wanted him.

The day's walk was long but relatively level. I was still tight and sore from the previous day, though. Fortunately, we stopped at a cool café, La Parada de Zurjain, along a river, for a mid-morning break. I thought Paul would have liked the river, robust and frothy, probably filled with fish. But no one I asked for help could twist off the lid of his mini-urn charm.

By the time we reached Pamplona, we were fully energized from the sun, from gaining physical strength as each journey stage passed, and most of all, from our wonderful international community. I had expected an introspective solo journey, but this was not the case. I had expected to feel left out of discussions of Catholicism but had not heard such religious discourse, although it may have existed in other social circles. The unexpected, what was developing, this inexplicable sense of comradery and optimism with my global counterparts, was perhaps what I needed more – especially in the Trump era, in a time of climate crisis, etcetera, etcetera – without even having realized it. Isn't it funny how sometimes the universe seems to know better than we, ourselves, do?

*

Before long, we were meeting Marianne and Michelle, who'd walked slower, in albergue Jésus y Maria, set in a restored church. We'd walked 20.9 km. After showers and naps, the Pinchos Pub Crawl in Pamplona began at Hemingway's protagonist, Jake Barnes' café, Iruña. Even without photos in front of me, I can picture the cavernous interior: green, arabesque columns like giant chess figures on a black-and-white checkered floor; mushroom tables; ornate ceilings and lighting; and the counter -- pinchos beneath glass – to the left as you entered. It was easy to imagine the setting of *The Sun*

Also Rises, replete with feathered flappers and hat-brimmed men, sharp in their suits.

The evening started with just us four. Marianne and Michelle split an order of pinchos and Pamela and I split another order, the Basque version of tapas, at each of the six café/bars we would visit, counterclockwise, around the main square. The cafés had awnings spanning buildings' width, covering outdoor seating. Pamela and I ordered a pincho that contained "hidden ingredients" and dubbed it our "mystery box." Beer went down easy. *Very* easy. Soon, we were collecting pilgrims at each new venue.

Marie from France joined us and recounted a story from the night before about these four American guys, likely recent college grad's, whom we'd all seen on our way to Zubiri and knew were there to party. They'd seemed nice enough. However, they'd had the audacity to return to the private albergue where Marie was staying, at 2 AM, loud and so trashed that one fell down the stairs. Another was discovered the next morning, naked and with a girl, sprawled out on a bench in a common area that pilgrims used for removing and storing hiking boots! We saw a different side of Marie – she was (rightfully) pissed! (Imagine Anne Hathaway scowling.) As the night wore on, the bench incident morphed into a running joke:

"Let's have shots! Anyone want Sex on the Bench?"

By the final bar, there were over a dozen of us. We'd taken a lovely group photo on a side street, learned more about each other's lives and countries, and had intimate conversations about such universals as illness and grieving. And, Pamela started smoking Michelle's cigarettes. (Pamela doesn't smoke.)

Marianne, Michelle, Pamela, and I all had to use the bathroom in this one cramped restroom. I was the only one who closed the interior door. "American!" Pamela accused, and we all laughed. (Yep, that's me, the prude!)

As folks started drifting away to albergues, a couple of lines from the *Sound of Music* song, "So Long, Farewell!" would tail them.

Most albergues have curfews, and if you don't return on time, you get locked out. Ours was 10:30, and Pamela decided about 10:15 that she just *had* to have pizza... and - off she went!

We'd been taking group photos on the albergue steps. I took a photo of the bench to the left and posted it to our WhatsApp thread, bearing the following caption: "I am a single bench, seeking two humans and some hiking boots."

Marianne, Michelle, and I entered the lobby, then stood just inside the door joking around, near the only employee on duty. Once she was in sight, we yelled, "Come on, Pamela, you can do it!" as she ran for the door the staff person was pulling shut.

Back Row: Fabi, Michael, Cort, Max, Alexander, Michelle, Marianne, Stacy, Kristen, Sonya, Theodore, and Lily Front Row: Stefan, Karen, Pamela, Me, Maria, and James

Three: Travel Tidbits

Resources

○ Picking up good city maps upon arrivals, even if layout is already included in your El Camino guidebook, is preferable. There's usually a difference in the amount of detail and degree of accuracy.

What Worked

○ Networking with locals about places to stay
○ Forming a WhatsApp thread, so that our international family could communicate regularly for free. We not only posted about social events but also each other's locations and such fun facts as whether or not a certain albergue should be avoided due to such undesirable elements as bedbugs. (Make sure to spray your sleeping bag with a good repellant before you leave home!)

What I'd Do Differently

○ Appreciate the usefulness of walking poles. I would never step foot on El Camino or another long trek again without a good pair.

Four

Exhaustion, Iglesias,
and Eating in Estella

The next day's hike would be the hardest. In our neighboring bunkbeds, Pamela and I had whispered and laughed with Marianne and Michelle as we wound down from our big night, getting only six hours of rest. I left the albergue with a disorganized pack and a disorganized mind. Before even reaching the outskirts of Pamplona, I took Excedrin. Then, we got lost, wandering for about 15 minutes before regaining our yellow shell arrows.

Shell directions, it should be noted, come in many forms and locations along El Camino, ranging from formal, official, and permanent; on stone tiles in the ground to yellow, painted shells arranged into arrows; to official insignia on walls or signposts; to simple, spray-painted yellow arrows. While the French Way is popular, in part, because it is the most well marked, finding shell markers can still be challenging at times.

Destined for Puente de Reina, 23.8 kms. away, we really had to push ourselves, since there was yet another mountain to climb, albeit smaller, with a rocky declivity.

It was actually a wonderful day. A fantastic breeze wafted that morning, and we passed fields of not just corn and wheat but also sunflowers and wildflowers. At a crossroad, we stopped to take a selfie together.

Midday, Pamela, who was holding up much better than I, put her arm around my shoulder, pointed to the mountain peak in the distance and, speaking slowly and softly as if to a preschooler, said, "You can see the top, Janine. Look – it's only *two inches* away!" She put her head close to mine, showing me the inches within the span of her thumb and index finger. "Come on, now, you can hike that - *just two inches!*"

We laughed so hard that we couldn't take a single step. Then, I took a deep breath, thought *two inches*, and double-timed my trudge.

Shortly, we reached the summit of El Perdón: yellow fields outlined in green foliage with a backdrop of mountains. An immense iron sculpture series – a train of pilgrims from different eras, called "Where the route of the wind crosses that of the stars" – reinforced El Camino's long history. A Great Wall of Windmills stretched out as far as we could see. A sign post indicated distances, arrows pointing every which way. We sat on a bench to rest and witness, trying to make the scene before us indelible in our minds' eyes. At various points along the Camino, I would absolutely ache for Mike and Jianna - the top of this magnificent range was one such time.

It was July 5th AKA "Death Day" to me because my mom had died 16-years' prior. Mom and I were close. She was my #1 fan and every child deserves such a mom. While the date no longer upset me, I still remembered it. Therefore, I dedicated my climb to Mom, which I told Pamela, adding, "The day Jianna was born, when the nurse first put her 6 lb. 12 oz. bundle in my arms, she yawned, and my first thought was that she looked like my mother." I continued, "It was such an unexpected and comforting initial thought – as though somehow in having my daughter, I'd reclaimed a little piece of my mom and would be taking care of her, too."

"I have a treat for you this afternoon!" Pamela's eyes shone.

Beneath the midday sun, we walked through a town where Basque architectural elements were incorporated into a modern neighborhood – the same tile roofs, same red shutters and trim. I loved this continuation of tradition.

Soon, we came upon Pamela's treat – the famous límonada stand!

A boy ran a stand for pilgrims and even had his own pilgrim stamp! I'd learned of it while researching. And there he was! The nice boy sat at his table, reading a book!

When we approached, I said, "I saw you on a video!"

He reddened slightly and smiled.

I purchased my beverage, handed him my passport, and attained my favorite stamp!

I later heard somewhere that he earned enough money selling lemonade to pay for his college education. I don't know if it's true, but I sure hope it is!

My usual short, quick clip, already slower, halved its pace as the day progressed, as if I were slogging through Lemon Jello beneath the unrelenting sun.

Finally, we reached Puente de Reina! Insult added to injury, the albergue was on top of a hill – we had to haul ourselves *up an incline* at the very end! Pamela had stayed there before, though. "It'll be worth it," she assured, "you'll see!"

And, she was right. We paid for a private room. It was my turn to sleep on the upper bunk, but there was no attached ladder, and I was too tired to swing my leg up high enough to make the climb, so Pamela volunteered to take the top. In fact, I was so tuckered out that for the first time since the trek began, I didn't immediately shower; although I felt disgusting, I crawled straight into bed and slept the sleep of the dead until just before dinner. (*Then*, I showered!)

Dinner at this more upscale albergue was good, and a bottle of wine was set at every table. Marianne and Michelle joined us and, sitting across from Michelle, I had a chance to get to know her better. She was a college student in Norway, and up until that point, she'd pretty much just made me laugh with her dripping sarcasm. When we actually talk-talked, though, I learned that she was an art and design student and about what lay ahead for her as she finished her degree. Our conversation provided a nice close to a very long day.

But, brain fog, headache, and exhaustion be damned – I wouldn't have changed a single thing about our Pamplona extravaganza!

*

Despite my nap, I slept soundly through the night and, before I knew it, we were off to the city of Estella. "Snail!" I called. It was painted on a fence but still counted.

"Fine!" Pamela grumbled. "I'll get the first beer."

(She'd found a snail on gravel a couple of mornings before and I'd had to buy.)

It had become a thing for us to pass an Asian couple or them us while the opposite duo was on break. En route to Estella, Pamela and I found ourselves trailside, sitting on our backpacks. Pamela had introduced me to these delicious límon sandwich cookies, and we'd made a habit of buying them whenever we saw them. She took a sleeve of the treat out of a pack pocket. "Cookie?" Pamela would offer to passersby, holding out the open package. Before long, this husband and wife we'd only exchanged nods with previously stopped and joined us. We chatted pleasantly for the first time.

Several additional Pilgrims had joined nos familia. Notably, Stefan, a father from Germany, who occasionally made funny faces or did a little dance; Fabi, a hilarious 23-year-old from Germany on his first international adventure and healing from a bad breakup with his high school sweetheart; Sophie, a young high school ESL teacher from Denmark; Emily, a young woman from Australia with bad gym shoes, whose feet paid the toll; and Valentine, a willowy 19 yr. old from Germany, who was always cutting sausage with a knife and popping slices into his mouth. In a town one day, I guessed that Valentine was "23"; he guessed I was "39." We were *both* delighted!

On we traipsed. Once in a while, Pamela would point out a historic church that she had already toured. She didn't mind resting on a bench or under a tree while I paid a quick visit. One that stood out had an exterior cloister – a feature that I'd never before seen. On this and other days, we would also cross stone bridges, some Romanesque, built as far back as the 11th century. I never ceased to marvel over the oldness or ornateness of these sites. It was akin to time travel.

This was the final day of my 40's. Silently, I let go of men, one by one, who had mentally, emotionally, physically, and/or sexually abused me. Relatives, science teacher, substance abusing ex-boyfriends, and a couple of drunk guys. I knew that I couldn't just step into 50 and forget – that kind of curative only happened in novels – but I was determined not to dwell. To stop flashbacks. No vile memories would be permitted audience to zap energy and joy from the second part of my life. I'd survived and returned to myself; I was blessed; I deserved better than their dead patches in my wild grasses.

My anxiety hasn't bothered me for days now. My and Pamela's feet crunched ground in harmony. *It's not perimenopause and not my heart – good to know. It's something I can learn to fight!*

We arrived in Estella. Like most Spanish cities, she was very old; she'd grown from village into city by the end of the 11th century – she was cobblestone, proud wooden doors, and stone buildings, yet abuzz with contemporary energy. We went straight to a pizza place that Pamela knew of where they cooked real Italian pizzas in a wood-burning stone oven. If there had been a straight Point A to Point B route, she'd have shot down it. She practically sprinted as it was. My personal pizza, sausage, onion, and artichoke, was the most scrumptious I've ever eaten, even having already visited Italy.

After checking into an albergue with a hippie commune vibe, and showering, we cut a narrow swath through guitarists and listeners to leave and explore the city. We visited Iglesia de San Pedro de la Rua and then Museo del Carlismo, both worthwhile, window shopping our way back to the albergue, next to a Pilgrims' hospital, which we counted ourselves lucky not to need.

We chose to have a quiet night, knowing that the next evening would be spent in Los Arcos, where we'd celebrate my big birthday with a "Paella Plaza Party." (Like the alliteration?)

Summit of El Perdón, Spain

Rooftop shot of Estrella

Four: Travel Tidbits

Resources

Mckarash, "The best lemonade stall." *Camino Santiago.*
    3 January 2021.https://www.caminodesantiago.me/
    community/camino-photos/the-best-lemonade-
    stall.6534/.

What Worked

- Purchasing quality hiking shoes was a bit of advice I'd
  heard repeatedly and followed. I chose hiking gym shoes
  since it was summer, took my time shopping at three locations, and purchased a good brand (Merrell) that felt
  just right on my feet. Even though I walked in them
  multiple times before the trip, as suggested, there never
  was a "breaking in" period – they felt great right from
  the start! I also followed the recommendation to buy
  footwear that is a half-size larger than you normally
  wear both because hiking socks can be thicker and feet
  tend to swell as the hiking day progresses.
- Researching how to avoid blisters, which can be a huge
  problem for pilgrims, also proved beneficial. While I
  had studied blister care and brought a blister kit, it was

the advice of a woman from the Chicago El Camino group that served me best. She swore by buying lightweight toe socks, so that toes don't rub together. Every morning, I'd put on a pair of toe socks, then don my regular hiking socks over them for extra padding. I only developed one small blister the entire trek, and I'm sure that having a little extra cushion under the balls of my feet didn't hurt either. I now swear by this method.

What I'd Do Differently

○ Plan more loosely. Scheduling tightly is a very American trait, I think, and I happen to be very good at packing as much as possible into a short time span because I believe that time is of the essence, and I don't have extended vacation time. This said, if I had given myself a little more wiggle room, Estella is a city I'd have spent an extra day exploring.

Five

Fifty!

I awoke at 5:35 AM to a "Happy Birthday" text followed by numerous Danish flag emojis from Marianne, which really made me smile. Pamela and I soon caught up with her and Michelle at a mercado with a picnic bench outside, where we ate our just-purchased breakfasts. The duo handed me a braided leather bracelet with a silver Camino shell decoration. It was very sweet of them! I snapped it onto my wrist.

By this time, I felt lighter – like the weight of adulthood had been lifted from my shoulders. When your only responsibility each day is to carry a backpack and walk along a well-marked path, and you go through towns on your way, stopping on streets and at outdoor cafés and restaurants to socialize, it's not unlike summertime during your teen years – those of beaches, bike rides, sports, and family entertainment centers. (Well, at least those are *my* memories.)

Anyway, this day was no different, and I felt even sunnier because it was my birthday and the *final day* of my trek. And - I would reach my goal destination without incident!

We took numerous breaks to socialize and rehydrate, more than usual, in fact. Except once, I hadn't found Coca-Cola Light in Spain. Luckily, I'd brought caffeinated gum and popped a piece in my mouth every morning first thing. I'd also discovered a blue sports drink, not unlike Gatorade, which helped to keep me hydrated, a nearly impossible task for us pilgrims. (We'd compared notes.)

Pamela and I stopped at a location that I knew from research existed and had been looking forward to experiencing – a pilgrims' fountain that provided a choice: water *or wine*! A sign in Spanish essentially read: "If you want to take Santiago, with strength and vitality of this great wine, take a drink and provide for happiness. Irache Fountain. Wine Fountain." There was a wine museum nearby, but it wasn't open yet. We soon hiked past stretches of abundant grape vines.

As we walked through woods, sun as the background color in a leaf mosaic, from behind we heard quick marching – and loud singing in English, "Happy Birthday to you, Happy Birthday to you…" Three long-legged pilgrims, including Sophie from Sweden, swiftly drive-by birthday hugged me and went on their long-legged way! I absolutely loved it! The birthday greetings continued as the day wore on. Unbeknownst to me, Pamela had excluded me on a WhatsApp thread, in which my birthday was announced, hence the unexpected revelry before the Paella Party even began.

Everything was going well, and we made it over yet another mountain, but then, the afternoon heat intensified, offering us no shade and no breeze. We all trudged, sometimes just Pamela and I, other times, talking with hikers who joined us. Pamela had loaned me both poles because my legs were acting up again. After an hour or two, we saw what I can only describe as a mobile home shell that had been split in half lengthwise - like a Fisher Price toy that you opened and set up. Multiple pilgrims gathered in the shade and rested in near silence. Even though it was open air, we could smell each other from the outpouring of sweat caused by the merciless sun. We were marinating in it.

After, our road wound around hills, and every time we rounded a bend, we hoped to see Los Arcos, but no luck. *This is it*, I would think, *this has to be it. I can't walk anymore.* We'd navigate a bend and then… nothing! I'd shuffle-limp some more. After all, it's not as though a pilgrim can actually sit down in protest and give up.

Finally – we spotted the Los Arcos sign! I DID IT! Pamela took a photo of me smiling while leaning against it. "Los Arcos" or "The Arches" – I'd chosen this town because it worked symbolically – I was walking through the archway into my fifth decade.

We checked into Peregrino Santiago about 2 PM. As we headed to our room, an older French woman I'd never seen before approached me, asking, "Are you the birthday girl?" When I said yes, she embraced me and did that fantastic two-cheek kiss that Europeans do.

This albergue was large and loud, with bedrooms connected like in a shotgun house. We would be staying in a quad and greeted our bunkmates. "Hola!" we exchanged with a Spanish woman, probably in her 60's, and her younger companion, who were on their way out of the door. Soon, we heard that the older of the two collapsed in the yard and was hauled off by ambulance. We hoped it was heat and not her heart.

Once settled in, I took inventory of my total Camino damage: sunburn, heat rash from ankle to just beneath the knee (something I'd never had before), one blister – *Not bad!* – and swelling of both knees (also new for me).

Pamela showered first and when she returned, she made me wear her slides into the shower because the floor was so wet and icky.

I think that Pamela and I had hoped for a repeat of our magical Pamplona night, but unlike our albergue, Los Arcos was quiet, and the skies grew gray, raining off and on. We still met for paella in the plaza: Pamela, Marianne and Michelle, Marie, Stefan, Fabi, Emily, Sophie from Denmark, Danny, and Katie from Canada. We sat beneath the umbrellas of pulled-together patio tables. The sweet, older man from Japan, whom I'd met on day one and we'd seen periodically since, hiking at a quick pace, also stopped by, took our photos, and had us write down our names for him, so he could match words to images.

I'd never eaten paella before and thought it good; however, experienced paella eaters weren't satisfied on my behalf, swearing there was better. Folks took turns buying me beer, and we chatted and laughed. But the simple truth is that the sun had done a number on us all and the evening was sedate by comparison to Pamplona. Even so, I was immensely grateful that mi familia internacional El Camino had come to celebrate with me and to say their good-byes! And, like in Pamplona, whenever anyone left, we sang the refrain from "So Long, Farewell."

I slept hard and still felt groggy the following morning as I packed. Pamela teared up when we parted. "Of my four Camino treks, this week with you has been the *best* one!"

We said we'd miss each other. (And we do!)

We'd already discussed plans to walk the Portuguese Camino for three weeks. For different physical reasons, neither of our husbands could hike long distances. Since we thought they'd get along fabulously, we envisioned them driving the route together and meeting up with us each evening.

Before spending three weeks together, though, we thought that Mike and I should hop a plane to the Dominican Republic and stay with them, so the hubbies could meet. I'd visit my friends in Haiti on the same trip. It was the perfect plan, and I couldn't wait to tell Mike!

I headed for the bus station, prepared for a long wait. Albergues stipulate early checkout times, so relaxing at mine had not been an option. While sitting on the bench, I thought about how each day the scenery had changed, always surprising, always lovely. Each day, the feel of the trek also transformed. Veteran Pamela said there were three legs to El Camino. Leg one, entailing the hardest terrain, broke you down physically. Leg two, the middle, broke you down emotionally. And the third leg re-assembled you, stronger. I only had time for leg one and was grateful that it had been the most physically difficult one. I'd learned that some pilgrims walked El Camino in sections; I hoped to one day return and begin anew, where I was leaving off in Los Arcos, perhaps with a young adult Jianna in tow, so that she, too, could have this amazing experience!

Arrival at The Arches!

Paella Plaza Party with Pamela, Michelle, and Marianne

Fabi, Stefan, and Sophie (Denmark)

Five: Travel Tidbits

Resources

Le Nevez, Catherine, et al., eds. *Discover Europe.*
    Lonely Planet, 2015.

What Worked

- Bringing caffeinated gum proved an expedient and inexpensive alternative to seeking a caffeinated beverage each morning
- Scheduling my bus and other return transportation reservations in advance

What I'd Do Differently

- Invest in a pair of lightweight, waterproof sandals, which would have served a dual purpose: walking around towns in something other than hot, heavy hiking footwear and wearing in shared shower stalls to prevent foot fungus. (I'd packed leather sandals, but they weren't designed for shower use.)

Six

Buses, Blur of Bulls, and Baguette

On the bus ride to Pamplona, I gazed out the window to the north and took in the distance that I'd hiked – approximately 100 miles in seven days. Unbelievable! It seemed so far of a walk as the vehicle practically retraced it, mile after mile. I knew that I would miss the Camino – orange poppies, lavender fields, olive groves, grape vines, sunflowers, roosters, owls, crickets. More so, the people.

I would soon arrive in Pamplona and walk to the uber-modern albergue with private sleeping pods that I'd reserved well in advance. Bed and storage were both inside the pod, along with a reading light, and once within, all a pilgrim had to do was slide the door down and – *wa-la!* – your own room! I'd never seen anything like it. The place was owned by brothers who were very warm and welcoming. When I entered, one was discussing chocolate-covered churros. The other slapped down a newspaper. "*This* is a chocolate-covered churro!"

It was a runner flying upside down, away from the horns of a black bull.

After checking in, I spent the afternoon roaming the city. Since San Fermín, an event dating back to the 3rd century, was a week-long, citywide festival with a "Running of the Bulls" each morning, everyone on every street, it seemed, was celebrating.

Most attendees had donned the traditional white apparel with red scarf and sash of the runners. Bands played along the streets – everything from Spanish to rock to xylophone and flute, people bursting into song and dance. A professional singer belted opera from a balcony to an ever-densening crowd.

I stopped for several minutes to watch a group of young revelers attempt to form a human pyramid. One row. Two rows. Three rows. *Come on, guys, you've almost got it*! By the time the final one went to balance on the tippy top, another 20-something in a lower tier had been handed his beer by an onlooking friend – since he wouldn't give up his alcohol and his limbs made a tripod instead of a quad – the whole structure collapsed like a kicked tent!

The square was filled with Jamaican immigrants selling souvenirs, costumed historical figures on horseback taking photos with children, and passed out revelers. Through the window of one bar, I saw boys dressed in white and red, sitting on kegs, legs dangling, watching the merriment.

In a park, I tracked down a statue of Ernest Hemingway, with a plaque: "Pamplona and Hemingway...Hemingway and Pamplona...They are inextricably linked..."

And, of course, I sampled more pinchos. (You would, too!) I took a couple photos and WhatsApped them to Pamela on a private thread to let her know that I was thinking of her.

Crowds grew into thick forests around my sapling-sized self and were harder to weave through as afternoon became evening. I had to give wide berth to a loud group performing outside of my albergue when I returned in order to reach the entranceway. Once inside, upon request, an owner gave me a map, marking what time I should leave the next morning and where I should go stand to best glimpse the Running of the Bulls.

I entered my pod. After stowing shoes and removing socks, I discovered that I had *no* ankles, none, nada – instead, "cankles" – due to sun and dehydration. Even so, I penned a journal entry, including: "Trip = confirmation of blessed life." Elevating my feet on an extra pillow, I fell asleep to the joyful noise of nearby music and merrymakers.

*

No – this can't be right! I was staring at the time on my cell phone. Quickly and quietly, I gathered my belongings and exited the dorm, went downstairs, readied for my day, and threw on my shoes. *How?* I realized that I'd set my alarm but, in my exhaustion, hadn't turned it on.

Off I set! So much spilled beer was stuck to the streets that my shoes said *rip, rip* every time I picked up a foot. It explained the necessity of tanker trucks with high-pressure hoses that I'd seen the previous afternoon.

I followed my map from the albergue owner, making the first several turns, when a young, drunk Spaniard pulled me into a parade being led by a band. He put his arm around me and had me dance down the street with him. I pumped my free arm, adding a hip wiggle and some rhythm. Several minutes' later, I wondered whether or not this party line was going to take me where I needed to go, so I ducked out. The Spaniard stopped and waited. I smiled and waved, and so did he.

I started reading street names and consulting my map. *There are too many people. Am I too late?* I wondered. *Should I try to make it back to the albergue to catch it on TV?*

Another young, drunk Spanish guy noticed me and my need for directions, so he wrapped his long arm around my shoulder and pointed around the corner. Following his tip, I ended up behind a wooden gate, with a great vantage point of the route. In fact, I had parked myself right next to a TV crew and watched them prep. The camera man was down on his belly on the cobblestone, filming a fake miniature bull. A few guys were already sitting on top of the gate. As with the prior day, the crowd was awash in white with red kerchiefs and sashes. An old, cigar-smoking Spanish man soon stood next me. In a deep, smoky voice, he chatted with everyone around him, including a preschooler – and me! I had to pull out my Spanish and, not close to fully awake, butcher my way through polite niceties. I suspected that if I were standing an eensy-bit closer, I'd be able to smell the alcohol on his breath. I had him pegged as a hard liquor man. As race time drew near, a guy sprinting from behind bolted up the fence in front of him, sat on top, and dangled his legs down directly in front of the old guy's face. He hurled Spanish up at the young buck, but the kid didn't budge. A few minutes' later, old guy nudged me and pointed, as if to say "watch this," and proceeded to tie the younger one's sash to the top bar of the fence, so that when he would leap up to cheer on the runners, he'd be yanked back down. But young buck caught him! The two exchanged fiery words and I could feel my anxiety start to ripen; however, the dialogue ended in laughs! I grinned at the duo.

Then, a woman with smeared mascara and a plastic cup of beer approached me, and we engaged in a stilted English conversation. Slurring, "Have a good life," and "Bulls are dangerous," she staggered on her way.

Race participants, male and female, mostly young, in bright and neon running shoes, jogged, jumped, and danced in place to warm up. One guy's t-shirt had pre-printed blood splatter already upon it. The noise level increased. A trickle began to jog.

Then, they were off! The race a flurry of red, white, and bull.

I'd only counted a few bulls as I watched, but once they passed, I reviewed the cell phone video I'd simultaneously shot. It showed that a whole herd of behemoths had rushed the runners! One scared racer even leapt halfway up a nearby wooden fence and swiftly hoisted himself over, rather than be gored.

After the blur of a race, I headed for the bus station. Several groups of young adults walked with their arms around one another's shoulders. Sticky streets were trash filled, and I'd occasionally stroll by someone off to the side, sleeping off the celebration. In some contexts, like nighttime in New Orleans, the scene might be unsettling, but during San Fermin, it had a great spirit. *No wonder Hemingway attended nine times!*

The water trucks were early birds, out spraying, prepping for the new day's crowd.

Upon arrival to the station, I entered the gift shop. An American guy with a bloody knee limped in while I was scanning cookbooks. The cashier handed him a first-aid kit from behind the counter. I bought a book on how to make pinchos.

Soon, I boarded a bus to the Biarritz airport and sat down next to a 34-year-old British fellow who'd just run, his knees scraped bloody, too.

"I was next to an Australian guy at the start, and we were talking," he reported. "We both took off running at the same time," (you don't start your mad dash until you see the bulls coming, you see) "and the Australian was gored! I wanted to go back to help him, but man…" he paused, replaying the scene in his head, "the sea of people just carried me away – there was no way…"

I was relieved to later read there were no fatalities that morning. (According to records kept since 1910, there have been 15 fatalities total.)

The Brit and I enjoyed conversing. He lived north of London and maintained that people are happier up there than in the city. Since I teach linguistics, we also discussed dialects. He said that where he lives, there's a group with a very distinctive dialect, yet 15 miles away, residents speak "the Queen's English." He was a professional abseiler/sub-contractor by trade who wanted to enter into abseiling for emergency rescue. While late to travel, he loved rappelling and other extreme sports. "The farthest I've been is Croatia," he said. "And this year, I quit my job, so I could explore Spain."

After the bus, a short plane ride, and another bus ride, I found myself in Paris. I tried desperately to make it to the Louvre before it closed at, I thought, 8 PM, but I'd mixed up the museum's late night, and even glimpsing the interior of the art museum for a half an hour was not in the cards. The glass pyramid entranceway was all I was going to be able to selfie. C'est la vie!

I crossed a bridge over the Seine into St. Germaine and had a delicious roast beef sandwich on a baguette along with my first French beer, 1664, at a café Hemingway had visited. I was in the historic left bank where Lost Generation artists like Gertrude Stein and Ezra Pound had gathered between world wars for stimulating conversation about the state of the world, literature, and other forms of culture. I envisioned my writer husband, artist daughter, and I in glitzy 1920's get-ups, chatting among them. *If only I could imagine it into fruition right now!*

Then, checking into my hostel, I smiled at a sign hung at registration: Under "Free Services," "guitars" (available for loan) was listed.

As Paris became blanketed in dusk, I took a stroll. Parisians on motor-scooters and bikes with woven baskets tooled by. After wending through a quaint neighborhood in the Montmartre quarter, filled with the hum of chatty folks seated outdoors at cafés, busy people watching, a scene sewn by strings of colored lights, I found myself climbing stairs. (I know that you won't believe me, but I have a theory that in Europe, staircases only go up.) I visited Sacré-Coeur. My niece the architect, who'd studied in France, had said, "Aunt Janine, the view from there is better than from the Eiffel Tower – and free!" so I slogged to the top to glimpse the magnificent white, domed basilica and gaze upon the magnificence below. By this time, night had curtained Paris. City lights sparkled. Onlookers flitted. Entrepreneurs sold cans of beer, sometimes straight from the cardboard case. Teen couples kissed.

Returning to the hostel, I paused to listen to a musician channel Bob Marley for a group of young adults, scene vibe imbuing me with hope.

Chocolate gelato tapped me on the shoulder before I reached "home."

Wearing of the traditional red and white, San Fermin
Festival, Pamplona

Human pyramid attempt

Hemingway's featured café, *The Sun Also Rises*

Six: Travel Tidbits

Resources

Steves, Rick. *Rick Steves' Spanish Phrase Book & Dictionary*,
3rd ed. Avalon Travel, 2013. (Please note that a
4th edition came out in 2019, so you may wish
to compare the two.) The work is lightweight,
pocket-sized, and focuses on tourist, including
emergency, phrases.

What Worked

○ Reserving an albergue well in advance of San Fermin

What I'd Do Differently

○ Purchase the red and white "uniform" of San Fermin to
feel more as though I fit in and been more in the spirit
of "When in Rome [or Spain]…"
○ Try even harder during and post-trek to hydrate and
hopefully avoid "cankles"

Seven

Sites, Surprise at Shakespeare, and Snails

I awoke that Tuesday to the sad fact that it was my only full day in Paris, my last one in Europe, and that I needed to make the most of it, despite cankles.

74

I already knew that what would have been my number one choice, the Louvre, was closed on Tuesdays (just my luck!), so I enacted Plan B, a recommendation from my mother-in-law, Wanda, and was standing in the Musée d'Orsay queue before the doors opened at 9:30. After indulging in a chocolate croissant in the café, I spent three hours blissfully strolling through galleries, examining works by Monet, Manet, Renoir, Picasso, Rodin, and other masters, as if in my own indestructible, silent bubble, although surrounded by many visitors. Renoir's cheery people welcomed. Rodin's Dante doorway warned. Van Gogh's textures projected dimensionality. A temporary exhibit of work by artists from Lithuania and surrounding countries voiced great suffering under oppressive regimes. Devils and the dying. Woman carrying boulder. Wraithlike gods staring and phantom children fading. Even the edifice, itself, was incredible – on the banks of the Seine, formerly the Orsay railway station, built for the 1900 World's Fair.

Sunny and in the low 70's, I took a long walk along the river, down Saint Michael Street, past kiosks where vendors sold books and art, to Shakespeare & Co. bookstore, across from Notre Dame. The scene was just like in paintings you see set along the Seine. I stopped to take photos of wooden yachts, for Mike, who loves boats. I ate a lunch of quiche and pink lemonade in the adjacent café. At a nearby table, I glimpsed an emerging writer being writerly. Impassioned, toiling, he scribbled away by hand. It made me smile.

I then stood in line to enter the historic book shop. Yes, in line. To get into a bookstore. In line!

I entered the main room and lo and behold – there it was! Mike's second novel, *Reincarnation Blues* – in a bookcase with a wooden ladder (a.k.a. a *real* bookcase!)! Even though you're not supposed to take photos, I furtively clicked twice, just that one shelf.

Worth the wait, Shakespeare & Co. was perfect! The store had nooks. And crannies. Mismatched, old, old bookcases with ladders, of course, and book cabinets with glass doors. A comfy space for naps dedicated to the bookstore cat. Images and names of early 1900's writers of renown who'd visited were painted on the wall along the stairs as I headed up to the poetry section – Hemingway among them. (Told you I stalked his ghost!) One section containing an acquired collection (not for sale) formed a reading library. And an old wooden bookstand swiveled, lazy Susan-style. Literary quotations hung over doorways like horseshoes. *If Mike and I came here together, we'd never leave! If there's a Heaven, please, please, let it be like this!*

When I left, I called my husband.

He picked up. "Is something *wrong*?!?"

I hadn't called him the whole trip, but I just *had* to tell him that the long famous ex-pat bookstore, Shakespeare & Company, carried *his* novel!

*

Crossing the river, I approached Notre Dame. Sadly, the line to enter the cathedral, fully beneath the penetrating afternoon sun, was too long for me and my swollen legs. Instead, strolling the perimeter, I took photos. Chyanne had instructed me, "Make certain to look at the flying buttresses." I rested on a park bench behind the great basilica, trying to etch every detail into memory. After, I walked around St. Germaine on the left bank again until I found a café that served Escargot – something I was determined to try before leaving Paris. (I remembered as a kid feeling *fancy* when I'd say "Escargot" or "Vichyssoise.") The waiter led me to a window seat, an elegant, upholstered booth for one with a petite mushroom table, facing Notre Dame; I had a great view of the gargoyles and could people watch at the same time. (Within two years, I would be grateful to have viewed the exterior before it was licked by flames!) I soon relished my six snails. A couple of tourists even came to an abrupt halt on the other side of the window to gaze at my plate; I'd response with a smile of perfect contentment. I'd started my meal with a bottle of 1664 and a bowl of French Onion soup; before I knew it, I was sopping up white wine and butter sauce with French bread.

*

Unfortunately, the situation took a bit of a downturn from there, but as they say, "All good things must come to an end." Exhaustion slammed into me and I started feeling sick, so I hailed a cab to return to the hostel. "Will you take me past the Eiffel Tower, the Arch de Triomphe, and Moulin Rouge on the way?" I asked the foreign driver.

We passed Moulin Rouge en route, and I tried to memorize its windmill blades and neon. The cabbie completely forgot my request, even though it would have meant a higher fare for him. I decided *not* to remind him because he was the craziest driver from whom I'd ever taken a ride – and I grew up in Chicago! The man actually honked pedestrians out of the way, and at one point, a male cyclist tapped on the window and yelled at him. I fastened my seatbelt.

At a busy intersection, he cut across FOUR lanes of traffic to his left to make a left turn. Horrified, I began to wonder if he even had a license! When my feet touched the sidewalk outside of my hostel, I nearly sank to my knees and thanked God.

I climbed the stairs to my empty room. My body then went into full-blown rebellion against my having pushed it relentlessly for nine straight days. After climbing into the top bunk, balcony doors wide open for the breeze, I watched the sun set. It just so happened to be the night of the futbol semi-finals, France vs. Belgium, and enough Parisians watched the game in local pubs and cafés that every time France scored a goal, I was made aware by the eruption of cheers.

Then - France won!

Into wee hours, I heard shouting, singing, and incessant horn beeping down the busy boulevard. It was as though France had been liberated from military occupation – I'd never experienced anything like it, even living in da backyard of da Bulls and da Bears! I would write in my journal, "Goodness knows how they're going to act if they win!" I couldn't know then that the French *would* win the World Cup against Croatia. The celebration would become riotous, fans vs. 110,000 security staff. They'd get so crazy reveling that one man would break his neck jumping into a canal and another would die, wrapping his car around a tree. Even later, I'd learn that in areas of the U.S.A., sports fans had exhibited equally riotous behaviors, and lives had been lost. I don't think it's something I'll ever understand. Whether bulls or more traditional sports, celebrations shouldn't lead to lost lives.

I enjoyed being bystander to the semi-finals revelry, though.

*

By the time I boarded my flight the next day, I could barely speak. From trekking princess to flying home frog, I croaked. As soon as possible, I converted my seat into a bed, wrapped my lily pad around me, and slept.

Mike and Jianna picked me up from the airport.

I handed them berets – classic black for Mike, fuchsia for Jianna, and red for me – perfect souvenirs for two writers and a budding artist!

When we entered the house, Jianna held up her "Welcome Home, Mother!" poster. I still have it.

View of Musee D'Orsay from the second floor

The famous bookstore frequented by Lost Generation writers

Seven: Travel Tidbits

Resources

Coulborne, Tanya, et al., eds. *Eyewitness Travel: France.*
    DK, 2016.

What Worked

- Getting verbal recommendations from previous tourists as well as Marie from Paris
- Reminding myself to "live in the moment" and "embrace the ecstatic experience"

What I'd Do Differently

- Research Notre Dame visitor's information and, considering the outdoor queue and weather, reversed the order of my day's adventure

Epilogue

I spent much of the next few days resting on the couch. Studying my legs, I began to wonder if I would ever see my delicate ankles again. *What if I've done permanent damage?* I wondered. Ridiculous, I know, but it's easy to be fearful when your legs suddenly resemble those of an elephant. Fortunately, the swelling soon abated. However, I would have laryngitis for several weeks.

Would I have pushed myself less had I known my legs would swell and I'd lose my voice? Nope. Not. at. all! I pushed myself on every hike and in every city because I wanted to make the most of the experience. I treat each travel adventure I'm fortunate enough to undertake as if I may never go that way again. The world is too vast for repeats when there is so much to explore! Every moment of my trip was worth the slight costs.

Pre-El Camino, I'd regularly had looping stress dreams. Usually, I was trying, unsuccessfully, to complete some mundane work task. Not only did I *not* have those stressmares for months post-El Camino, but also, the dreams that did visit were blissful. At the beginning, they were set on El Camino, and I'd awaken elated! And, despite living in the era of Trump, my "inner-flutteriness" did not return for months. In fact, I rode my newfound sense of calm and reinvigorated belief in humankind like a wave well into the shoreline of my fall semester of teaching. It was lovely! I wish I could say that I discovered a way to make the feeling of well-being permanent – but if I claimed that, I'd be writing fiction. Yet, the trip made me see what is possible – it gave me hope.

While at the airport waiting for my family to pick me up, I read my friend Kirk's email. He wanted to know if I would be interested in picking up a creative writing class at his university for fall. Little did I know that it would lead to lasting work, where I love my students and can actually concentrate on teaching. From that fall forward, I've been blessed to have one foot in academia and the other in freelancing – solid, lush ground.

I kept track of the continued journeys of my international community of friends on our WhatsApp thread, missing and cheering them on. In early August, numerous pilgrims posted photos of their arrival at the cathedral of Santiago de Compostela in Galicia, on the northwestern coast, where the remains of the apostle, Saint James the Great, were presumably enshrined.

Pamela and I continued to message on a private thread, comparing notes and laughing.

However, this laughter ceased with one early August text and wouldn't return for a long while.

Pamela never made it to Compostela. While she was hiking, her husband, Cliff, was involved in a car accident in the Dominican Republic. He died soon after, alone in a hospital room, in a country he'd only called home for eight months. He was 51.

For Princess Pamela, it was like her personal field of sunflowers had been macheted.

I couldn't believe that I had grieved the death of Paul, Pam's husband, on El Camino, only to become friends with a Pamela who would, in turn, lose her Cliff – both husbands gone too soon.

Our closest group members, especially Marie, who could most relate, would send as much love and strength to Pamela as we could muster in the months to come as she endured a nightmarish process involving emergency travel to the DR only to learn she was too late, cremation, selling her salon, and attaining permission to transport the ashes to Canada where she returned to be near sisters and mend. She had to face the questions that Marie struggled with before, during, and undoubtedly still after her journey: *Who am I without my husband? How do I re-envision my life?*

During a recent group Zoom conversation, it became clear that in such grief work, both widows realized they would never be the same. When someone close to you dies, you aren't, after all, meant to remain untouched. Loss and sustained love inform character, perspective, becoming integral. As Marie would say, "There is a hole, but it becomes smaller with time. If you need to, you build a fence around it, and continue with life." Pamela is strong. Like many women, myself included, she was made stronger than a woman should ever have to become. She's starting to grow new flowers.

Paul's wife, Pam, and his boys plodded onward as well. Matthew continued college, grades steadily improving, internship in the summers. Joshua joined the National Guard and completed basic training; the following year, he graduated from high school. Paul would be (is?) very proud of his wife and sons.

Sigh... Paul still won't come out of his urn necklace. I occasionally hold the capsule and update him on the ongoings of his family and tell him how much I still miss him and that he isn't forgotten.

The WhatsApp thread continues. Photos of Spanish Tortilla making have been relegated to the past by holiday wishes, photos of Sonia's boys getting taller, the Germans visiting one another, and Emily from Australia's wedding. Folks checked in "safe" as the Pandemic began to rage. More recently, Fabi posted a photo of his Camino in Germany's Black Forest.

Next scheduled Zoom meeting? A celebration of Pamela's 50th birthday!

When Marianne, Michelle, Camila, Marie, Pamela, and I video chat, sentences overlap in our rush to catch up; we talk and laugh like no time has passed. Marianne remains cancer free. Michelle graduated from college and is applying to graduate school; she's moving into a house filled with artists and has an art trip to Germany planned. Camila is drawing her Camino as a book. Marie made an announcement. She met a Canadian, Michael, on El Camino, and they have fallen in love.

We know we will see one another again.

Notes

Kepnes, Matthew. "Nomadic Matt's Tuesday Travel Update." 25 August, 2020.

pg 3. "St. Jean Pied de Port: Gateway to the Camino Frances." *Camino Ways*, 24 February, 2020,

   https://caminoways.com/st-jean-pied-de-port-gateway-french-way.

pg 9. "Bayonne." *Lonely Planet*, 2021, https://www.lonelyplanet.com/france/southwestern-

   france/bayonne

pg 48. "Estella." *Vive el Camino*, 2021, https://www.vivecamino.com/en/estella

pg 68. "Running of the Bulls Deaths." The Running of the Bulls, 2021,

   https://www.runningofthebulls.com/history-of-the-bulls/running-of-the-bulls-deaths/

JANINE HARRISON teaches creative and freelance writing at Calumet College of St. Joseph and American Public University and is a freelance writer and a teaching artist. A former Highland (IN) Poet Laureate (2017-18), she wrote *Weight of Silence* (Wordpool Press, 2019) and *If We Were Birds* (Moria Books, 2017). She also co-wrote the joint memoir, *An Irish Love Story*, with Tom and Jean Burns. Her travel writing, poetry, and short prose have been published in numerous magazines and anthologies. Janine has been a featured writer at literary events around the Midwest. She volunteered as a literary not-for-profit organization leader and a poetry reader and reviewer for *The Florida Review*. Born in Chicago and raised in a south suburb, she lives in Northwest Indiana with her husband, fiction writer Michael Poore, and teen digital artist daughter, Jianna Sol. Janine loves to travel, experiencing other cultures and serving when she is able. Visit her at janineharrison.com, and follow her on Facebook @Janine.Harrison.75 and Instagram @southpawscribbler.

9 780578 894454